EARTHQUAKE
7.1 San Francisco Bay Area
October 17, 1989

LTA Publishing Company
Publisher - Sponsor
United Press International
Co - Sponsor

Concept & Design: Robert D. Shangle, LTA
Photo Laboratory and Library Services
provided by UPI/Bettmann News Photos
News Material: United Press International
Edited by: Barbara J. Shangle, LTA
24-Hour Color Separation Service by
Toucan Scan, Portland, Oregon

Publishing by LTA Publishing Company
2735 S. E. Raymond Street
Portland, Oregon 97202
(503) 238-2551
ISBN 1-55988-120-8

Printed in the United States of America

EARTHQUAKE
7.1
San Francisco Bay Area
October 17, 1989

San Francisco, (UPI),

By Arthur McGinn, *October 17, 1989*

A major earthquake struck northern California Tuesday night, killing at least 50 people, knocking out power, starting fires, and collapsing buildings, freeways and a section of the Bay Bridge. The quake postponed the World Series.

The earthquake struck during the rush hour and a half-hour before Game 3 of the World Series was scheduled to start at Candlestick Park in San Francisco. Players and their families rushed onto the safety of the field. Some of the 68,000 fans said the park shuddered under the rolling motion.

At least six people were killed in San Francisco when a brick building collapsed. Some of the victims were in cars crushed by falling bricks, police Lt. Jerry Kilroy said. A seventh person was confirmed killed in the collapse of a section of the upper roadway of the double-deck Bay Bridge.

The rolling quake along the notorious San Andreas fault struck at 5:04 PDT and lasted about 15 seconds. At least two aftershocks were felt. Caltech seismologists in Pasadena estimated the quake at between 6.5 and 7.0 on the open-ended Richter scale. Russ Needham, geophysicist of U.S. Geological Service in Golden, Colorado, said the quake had a magnitude of 6.9. A magnitude 7 is considered a major earthquake capable of widespread, heavy damage.

There were several fires burning in downtown San Francisco, including one covering a city block in the Marina District, and across the bay in Oakland and Berkeley. Some cars were trapped or crushed beneath a downed section of the Bay Bridge, which links San Francisco and Oakland. Officials said at least one person was killed in the collapse.

In Oakland, a half-mile section of the upper deck of Interstate 880 collapsed. The Embarcadero Freeway, an elevated double-decked roadway that runs along the city's waterfront, also sustained some damage and was shut down. In addition, the San Mateo, Carquinez and Richmond-San Rafael bridges were closed off for inspection.

The Bay Area Rapid Transit system that runs below San Francisco Bay and beneath the city streets was shut down. One train in a tunnel through the Berkeley Hills was evacuated.

"It felt like one of those huge monsters from a Japanese horror movie grabbed a hold of the building and was shaking the hell out of it," said Margi Cornehl, a city planning employee in San Jose, 50 miles south of San Francisco, who was working on the fourth floor of the six-story City Hall.

Santa Cruz, Ca., (UPI),

By Carrick Leavitt, *October 18, 1989*

Two people were killed and a third was presumed to have died Tuesday in Santa Cruz, about 10 miles southwest of the epicenter, three were killed in San Jose and one each in the smaller communities of Capitola and Watsonville.

Electricity and gas service were cut off throughout Santa Cruz County, and residents were warned to boil drinking water for fear supplies may have been contaminated by broken sewer lines.

Fires, many caused by leaking natural gas and downed power lines, destroyed 60 homes in Santa Cruz County and triggered several grass and brush blazes, the largest about 65 acres at the Nisene Marks State Park in Aptos, said Dan Turner, assistant fire chief for the California Department of Forestry. A total of 1,100 firefighters from the state and from surrounding counties were snuffing the blazes, Turner said.

A county official reported 75 percent of the mobile homes surveyed, of the southern county, were knocked off their supports.

Two of those killed in the seaside community were crushed in the collapse of a number of stores at the historic Pacific Garden Mall in downtown. Officials said they feared additional victims were buried under the massive piles of brick and glass.

No precise injury figures were available, but at Dominican Hospital, the sole Santa Cruz-area hospital that treated patients overnight, 85 people were treated and 26 were admitted, officials said. A total of 40 buildings collapsed throughout Santa Cruz County, but all hospitals were open, officials said. At least 358 people in Santa Cruz were provided overnight shelter at six emergency centers.

Megan Morgan, who helped dig out a woman buried in the collapse of a building, said she ran to the Pacific Garden Mall to help look for friends. "We dug through debris, brick and plaster, until we reached her. She had no pulse, nothing," Morgan said.

Property damage in the city was estimated at $350 million.

Rockslides closed roads in the area, including Highway 17 between Santa Cruz and San Jose. A northern route out of Santa Cruz, Highway 9, remained open through Great Basin State Park, but Highway 1, the coastal highway, was closed at the Green Valley Road overpass.

The epicenter of an earthquake that virtually shut down San Francisco, 60 miles to the north, shook again early Wednesday at 3:25 a.m., with an aftershcok that measured 4.5 on the Richter scale. There was no immediate word of additional damage or injuries.

In other damage:

In Hollister, 35 miles east of Santa Cruz and the closest community to the center of the quake, the city was thrown into confusion. More than 40 houses were rocked off their foundations, downtown buildings were damaged and the roof of the J.C. Penney building collapsed. There were no deaths but 49 injuries were reported. A third of the 17,000 residents were without running water and officials worried supplies may be contaminated.

In Watsonville, buildings sustained heavy damage and several brick structures collapsed. Some 1,500 to 2,000 frightened residents spent the night sleeping in parks or schools.

In Salinas, city officials declared a state of emergency after an underground gas tank ruptured beneath the Lawrence Expressway, pouring gasoline into storm drains.

In San Jose, the California Highway Patrol flew in 500 pounds of blood by helicopter for the hundreds of casualities. Three deaths were reported in the city. Downtown buildings were damaged, including the 11-story California Commercial Bank building.

In Sunnyvale, an apartment complex was hit by an explosion triggered by a buildup of gas; another building was damaged by a boiler explosion.

Oakland, (UPI),

By William H. Inman, UPI National Reporter, *October 20, 1989*

A shocked and deeply moved President Bush inspected the damage from this week's killer earthquake Friday and called the father of a young boy whose leg was amputated to free him from a car containing his dead mother.

Gov. George Deukmejian told the president there would be requests for more federal financial aid in the aftermath of the quake, which killed at least 63 people.

Bush was greeted by Deukmejian when he arrived at Moffett Naval Air Station near San Jose at about 8:30 a.m. then was briefed by local officials, including San Francisco Mayor Art Agnos.

A helicopter took him up San Francisco Bay and he landed on the Oakland side of the Oakland Bay Bridge near the collapsed two-tiered stretch of Interstate 880, where most of the earthquake fatalities occurred.

"Jesus," he said when he first saw the mile-long stretch of the freeway, which buckled and collapsed in places.

"I was deeply moved by it," Bush said. "I had feelings of contradictions, one of great sadness (and) of genuine appreciation for the way this community is pulling together."

Bush lauded the efforts of the military, local, and state officials. His trip down the block was cut short because engineers would not let him go underneath the highway, fearing it might collapse.

While in Oakland, the president made a telephone call to Pastor Berumen, the father of Julio, 6, and Cathy, 8. The children were rescued from the wreckage of their mother's car in a dramatic incident that required a doctor to amputate Julio's right leg.

The children's mother and another woman in the car were killed.

"I'm proud of your courage, proud of the doctors," Bush told Berumen. "You be strong."

Carrying a hard hat and followed by area congressmen, Bush walked down the street talking to police officers, and later headed south of San Francisco and Oakland to Santa Cruz, near the epicenter of the quake.

"God bless those volunteers," Bush said in Santa Cruz, talking about the Red Cross and others helping to clean up the disaster area. Five died in the seaside community.

Bush, a strong advocate of volunteerism, said, "There's no ceiling on the compassion of the American people."

Bush said on departing from California Friday evening that "we're going to do what is necessary to fix it."

"It's been a very moving day," the president said.

As of Friday evening, 45 bodies had been recovered from the remains of the two-level Oakland freeway, Alameda county authorities said.

The final death toll may not be compiled for some time, but most feel it will be much lower than initially believed. Authorities have located only 52 vehicles, 31 of which contained bodies.

"It can take up to three months to take (the crumbled section) down and haul it away," Carl Nelson, a spokesman for the state Transportation Department said late Thursday. "The pancaked section is a total mystery."

Initial projections that the quake killed a total of up to 273 people appear to have been inflated because of the flawed initial estimates of the number dead in the Oakland highway collapse.

Nature was not being kind to the Bay Area. Rain was expected to pelt the quake scene by late Friday, raising the threat of mudslides, especially in the hilly areas of Santa Cruz County already ravaged by the killer quake.

San Francisco, (UPI),

By William H. Inman, UPI National Reporter, *October 19, 1989*

Hundreds of patients were evacuated Thursday from two hospitals cracked by the nation's second-deadliest quake. In Palo Alto, 30 miles south of San Francisco, 250 patients were evacuated from psychiatric and medical units of the Veterans Administration late Thursday. "We had noticed interior cracks in the buildings," Darrell Davis said. "We ordered teams to check the integrity of the buildings." The patients were taken to other VA facilities, Davis said.

Excavation work, meanwhile, centered on a crushed mile-long double-deck highway in Oakland. . . . Firefighter Daniel Getreu pulled out the body of a woman and child. "They were dirty. They were crushed. And they were dead," he said. "There was a space of about one-and-a-half feet from the top of the car to the bottom. We pulled the windshield back and a child's book was stuck to it," he said. "The windshield was pressed to that baby." He said "dozens of bodies" were trapped in the 100 yards of ferroconcrete he was searching. "There are lots more (bodies)," he said. "I'm all burned out."

Aftershocks rippled across northern California, though none was as powerful as the initial temblor, which measured 6.9 on the Richter scale. Thursday's aftershocks, which included a 3.0 shaker shortly after 5 p.m. PDT, registered as high as 4.67 on the open-ended scale.

Lloyds of London, the insurance underwriting group, placed damage at $5 billion in downtown San Francisco alone. City officials had placed damage at $2 billion.

The Oakland coroner's office received offers from meatpackers volunteering to store corpses in refrigerated meat lockers. In addition, funeral parlors were preparing for quick, cut-rate services. "We've had offers from a number of different companies and meatpackers," said Sgt. Donna Jay, a spokeswoman for the city coroner's office. "We put the names on a resource list and we can go to them for help if we need them."

By Thursday, power and water had been restored to most sections of San Francisco. Aid continued to flow from around the world, the latest offer from Israel, promising search-and-rescue teams. Even the Michigan Chiropractic Society offered to chip in.

Early Thursday, 42 hours after the quake, an aftershock measuring 4.6 on the Richter scale struck the riverfront city of Santa Cruz, according to the National Earthquake Information center in Golden, Colorado. A second aftershock, estimated at about 3.7, toppled a 79-year-old Watsonville church steeple damaged in Tuesday's quake, the Santa Cruz County Office of Emergency Services said. County authorities scrambled into the nearby mountains to determine if newly discovered fissures, one 4-feet wide, threatened homes in the area. An assessment of damage in the county showed 280 homes destroyed in the quake and another 80 homes uninhabitable, the office said.

Oakland, Ca., (UPI),
October 18, 1989

A six-year-old boy was rescued from beneath tons of concrete rubble as police and firefighters worked to determine how many died under an elevated highway brought down by the massive earthquake that struck the San Francisco Bay area. Firefighters, looking for survivors and trying to locate the dead, moved alongside the flattened structure and heard the cries of the boy.

The child was trapped when a quake measuring 6.9 on the Richter scale struck Tuesday evening, causing an 18-block segment of the top level of the double-decker Interstate 880 freeway to collapse and crushing "several hundred cars" beneath, Oakland Fire Department District Chief Al Sigwart said.

The boy, whose leg was amputated to free him from a demolished car, was reported in extremely critical condition Wednesday at Children's Hospital in Oakland after his nearly seven-hour ordeal. He was not immediately identified and authorities were referring to him only as John Doe.

The concrete beam had crushed the front of the car in which he was a passenger, killing his mother instantly and injuring his sister. The impact caused the boy to slide forward between the two front bucket seats, where his right leg was pinned.

The boy's sister, known only as Jane Doe, 8, was removed immediately and taken to Eden hospital in Castro Valley with head, face, and abdominal injuries.

Dr. Jack Ellis, 30, one of five physicians who operaterd on the boy, said the child was conscious and speaking Spanish when they arrived on the scene. Once they saw the leg, they realized they would have to amputate it to save him, he said. But the operation to amputate the leg and free the boy did not end until midnight, nearly five hours later.

San Francisco, Ca., (UPI),
By John M. Leighty, *October 19, 1989*

There is a new wave of homeless people in San Francisco, hundreds of residents forced out of their damaged or collapsed homes and apartments in the posh Marina district near the Golden Gate Bridge. Temporarily, they are finding adequate food and shelter at the Marina Middle School, where the community spirit has been prevailing over what otherwise could have been a crushing blow for residents, many of them elderly and living in rent-controlled apartments they may never see again. Some, who escaped with only the clothes on their backs, are worried about what will happen to them once the influx of volunteers leave and life in the city begins to return to normal.

One elderly man, Leo Attar, has lived in his Marina district apartment for 45 years, originally paying $75 a month in a space that would now bring $1,400, about $1,000 more than he's paying. A sign on a door of his 3-story apartment reads: "Unsafe. Do Not Enter." Now, he says, his future is unsure. He doesn't even know if he'll be able to retrieve his belongings, which were strewn about when the earthquake hit. "I've seen many homeless people come to San Francisco and the city has tried to help them. I think it's remarkable. Now I could be one of them, I don't know."

Depending on damage, some 40 to 50 buildings in an 8-block stretch of the Marina could be uninhabitable for months, and many may be torn down. Residents were given badges by a police damage assessment team Thursday that would allow them either to go back to their living spaces, go in to get belongings, or remain in shelters because of the dangers.

Although the Marina district school may soon have to close as an emergency shelter to reopen for junior high classes, Police Chief Frank Jordan assured the homeless that four alternate sites were available, including one run by the Salvation Army.

Santa Cruz, Ca., (UPI),
By Carrick Leavitt, *October 20, 1989*

Jim and Sheryl Pattison barely looked up from the charred ruins of their home Friday when a helicopter carrying President Bush soared overhead and landed on a nearby dirt air strip.

The Pattisons' mountain home survived the big shaker Tuesday and the family had been using a woodstove to boil creek water and cook for themselves and quake-stricken neighbors. But their house was destroyed by flames after a jolting aftershock 48 hours after the initial temblor.

Bush left the presidential helicopter and motored 6 miles down Highway 17, buckled and cracked by Tuesday's 6.9 magnitude quake, to visit the shopping mall where three people died under collapsed stores.

But, 2 miles off the highway, up the twisting Lockhart Gulch Road not far from the quake's epicenter, the Pattisons and their three children had little thought for the chief executive's disaster tour. Their $175,000 wood frame home went up in smoke following the 4.3 magnitude aftershock that rattled the area at 5:18 p.m. Thursday. "I can't believe it. There isn't anything left," said Sheryl Pattison, 38, a computer operator, as she got the first good look at the destruction in daylight Friday.

The family wasn't home when the fire broke out and it was too dark to inspect the damage when they arrived back there Thursday night. The only things salvaged by firefighters were a blackened teddy bear, a yellow rubber duck, and a clothes hamper. "The real loss is all the pictures and scrapbooks we saved for the kids," said Jim Pattison, 39, as he contemplated the ruins. "The little things we've collected as the years go by, pictures of the kids being born, records of their growing up, things that happen, we took family pictures every year. They're all gone."

Pointing to one charred section, he added, "The dining room table was grandma's. It was the first thing we had when we were married. I was hoping some of these things would be left."

He said the chimney blew off their house when the major earthquake struck Tuesday, knocking furniture about and putting a 2-inch crack along a section of the home. Since their son, Dale, 5, just contracted the chicken pox, they couldn't stay with neighbors, so the family of five slept together on a big waterbed and considered themselves lucky.

They were doing well until the aftershock, which either knocked something on the woodstove, which was hot, or caused an electrical short-circuit. Power had just come back on after being knocked out since the quake.

The Pattisons daughters, Christine, 9, and Jennifer, 8, sifted through the rubble and cheered when they found a toothbrush and an encyclopedia intact. "I don't know what the heck I'm going to tell Mr. T., my teacher," said Christine. "He's not going to believe my excuse when I tell him my house burned down and I don't have my homework."

The family was among an estimated 8,000 people left homeless in Santa Cruz County, according to county supervisor Garry Patton. He said many people are camping out and that officials have requested tents and supplies from the Fort Ord Army base and the National Guard. "A real concern is the overcast skies and predictions of rain and what will happen to people," he said.

Damage to structures in the county was estimated at $525 million, including $400 million to private residences. The figure was expected to climb as structural inspections continue.

County officials said there had been 140 fires in the county since the earthquake struck Tuesday, including brush and fires. At least 2,000 people sought shelter in churches, armories, and Red Cross facilities.

The Pattisons, meanwhile, gathered to eat in a local restaurant, with Sheryl uttering a prayer, "Thank you, Jesus, that we are all alive and safe. Thank you for what we have." A waitress, tears in her eyes, told them there would be no charge for their meal.

San Francisco, Ca., (UPI),
By Pamela A. MacLean, *October 18, 1989*

Survivors of California's most deadly earthquake since the legendary temblor of 1906 gathered on the city's highest hill to gaze at a skyline doused in darkness and give silent thanks for their lives. Scores of San Franciscans scaled the 950-foot Twin Peaks as darkness fell and shrouded the mayhem done by Tuesday's powerful quake. They knew the lovely view of San Francisco's famous skyline, illuminated only by a three-quarter moon hanging over the city, was but small consolation for the knee-quivering fear they had just experienced and the tragedy suffered by many of their neighbors. But they came anyway, as if to find something of beauty and escape the disaster.

Mark Dayton, 29, of Oakland, said he rushed out of a building after feeling the tremors and learned that a nearby brick wall had collapsed and killed several people. "The block looked like a sea serpent. The street was undulating," he said. "It was amazing to see the street going in so many directions at once."

For a long time, as the survivors watched from the hill that is normally a lovers' retreat, the only lights in the city were those from hospitals and a few other buildings with emergency generators. Then, slowly, the city lights returned, section by section, as cheers drifted up the hill from the neighborhoods below. Down in the city, things did not seem so peaceful.

A huge fire gutted a square block in the Marina district late Tuesday. Nearby Lombard Street was a montage of sirens, smoke, and helicopter search lights. Sirens wailed in the air as emergency crews were pushed to the brink and helicopters landed within blocks of City Hall. What was once only a plan on paper had turned into an earthquake command center.

People clustered around phones trying to reach loved ones. Others played flashlights on buildings, revealing cracks and other damage. Pizza parlors and delicatessens operated by candlelight, with lines of people extending out the doorways.

The earthquake struck a half-hour before Game 3 of the World Series was scheduled to start at Candlestick Park in San Francisco. Players, their families and many of the 60,000-plus fans rushed onto the safety of the field as the stadium shuddered under the rolling motion. United Press International staff writer, William Murray, said many baseball fans kept remarkably cool. "Phones immediately went out and the sky went dark from power outages," Murray said. "But no panic swept the stands. Fans stood looking at each other wondering what to do."

San Francisco, Ca., (UPI),

By William H. Inman, UPI National Reporter, *October 18, 1989*

In the shadow of San Francisco, the "cool gray city of love," beneath a mountain of slag and concrete, 6-year-old Julio Berumen lost his mother and his right leg. He was in a car funneling north through the lower tier of the Nimitz Freeway near the Bay Bridge linking Oakland and San Francisco when crustal plates of the Pacific and North America nudged each other.

Scientists call it a strike slip.

It was Tuesday, 5:04 p.m. The third game of the nearby World Series was about to begin. The sun was shining. But the lights dimmed for Julio. The highway's upper-deck supports snapped like matchsticks. The seismic hiccup carried a force of 2,000 kilotons of TNT. Nimitz was a stone sarcophagus. Julio was inside.

Julio's story was horrific but typified the ordeal of the Bay Area, a place of poets and pleasure now cleaning away the detritus of nature's death blow. The San Francisco area, a patchwork of communities of 5-million people, was hammered by a quake registering 6.9 on the Richter scale, a fairly moderate disturbance by geological standards. Mexico City's 1985 temblor registered 8.1, meaning the ground motion was roughly 100 times greater. Eight thousand died. Last year's Armenia shaker, also 6.9 on the Richter, killed 25,000, the extraordinary toll blamed on primitive construction. The same seismic movement that set off the big 1906 San Francisco quake, 8.3 Richter, 700 dead in the quake and fire, killed 20,000 in distant Valparaiso, Chile.

But Tuesday's quake was different. A freak of timing and geography made it one of history's memorable shakers. "If this disturbance had struck in the Canadian wilderness with 10 times more force, it would be a scientific notation, not the cataclysm it became," said Art Lerner-Lam, a seismologist at Lamont-Doherty Geological Observatory in New York. "But this hit in a densely populated area when the eyes of the nation were focused here."

In fact it was the height of baseball season. The nation caught first glimpses of the fire sweeping San Francisco's Marina District from cameras mounted aboard the Goodyear blimp hovering over Candlestick Park.

It took only 30 seconds. It began at a fork of the San Andreas Fault, the boundary of continental plates, somewhat near a wilderness mountain called Loma Prieta, 60 miles south of San Francisco. In Spanish, Loma Prieta means dark hill.

Ripples moved concentrically. The first hit took place in a retirement community, Capitola, 10,000 population. One woman died of a heart attack. Chimneys fell. In nearby Santa Cruz, quaint shops and riverfront homes, 32,000 people, was gutted. Shaking intensified on the coastal alluvial deposits, turning clay to mud. Five died. One was killed when his car struck crazed horses on a highway. Los Gatos, population 22,000, 50 miles from San Francisco, lost power, gas, and water. In the Silicon Valley's Cupertino, a 77-year-old man died of heart failure.

Injuries and damage swept up the sandy headland toward San Francisco. At Candlestick Park, jammed with 62,000 fans, cracks opened in the turf. Players dashed from dugouts. The crowd initially mistook the 30 seconds of rumbling for foot stomping. They cheered. Then fell quiet. Surprisingly, the longest lines were not at the exits, there was no panic, they were at the stalls selling beer and pretzels.

Loma Prieta thundered into San Francisco, shaking loose windows from skyscrapers, snapping power lines, and trembling monuments. At the Edwardian St. Francis Hotel, the Viennese grandfather clock stopped. It kept good time through the 1906 quake. The Marina District, stucco villas on reclaimed land, suffered the brunt. Gas lines broke and flames licked the pierfront.

The affluent joined the homeless. Eight people died of fire and falling wall. A section of the "quake-proof" Bay bridge was ungirded and swallowed a motorist. Major arteries were made impassable, power disappeared, phone service turned erratic and the economic life of the wall street of the West fled.

But it was across the bay that the real terror surfaced. It came on the mile-long stretch of Nimitz . . . one of California's oldest double-decker [roadways]. Ten years ago engineers recommended the span be made stronger by replacing the Eisenhower-era supports with a core of steel in a spiral, rather than in parallel, formation. The spiral design wraps tightly around the concrete, reinforcing it. The older, parallel design permits the core to break apart when jolted by the varied stresses of an earthquake. The recommendations of the engineers were not taken. Nobody knows, or is willing to say, why.

As predicted, the highway's upper-tier supports popped like firecrackers, one after another. And one after another, 500-ton sections of the Nimitz Freeway thudded down on unlucky travelers below. Some cars were left intact, abandoned by their owners. Some cars were crushed to a height of $1^{1}/_{2}$ feet. The governor said he was "disappointed" by the structure's collapse, and both he and Oakland's mayor called for an investigation.

There were thousands of known casualties; at least 2,750 people were treated by 112 hospitals; but nobody knows the death count and probably won't until the last section of the Nimitz span is lifted.

Indeed the Bay Area has shown remarkable powers of recuperation. Power was restored within two days. Water mains were patched. Looting was kept to a minimum, although thieves were the first on the scene at the Nimitz disaster, filching watches and wallets and making identification more difficult.

Police, firefighters and volunteers from all walks worked 20-hour days. Streets were cleared of rubble and trolleys soon resumed their routes. Residents opened their homes to the homeless, some shelterless before Loma Prieta. Aid and offers of aid poured in from as far away as Israel and from groups as diverse as brewery workers and chiropractors.

San Francisco, Ca., (UPI),
By Robert Strand, *October 18, 1989*

Earthquakes, like other disasters, elicit the best and the worst in people. When the ground stopped shaking, many offered their help; others took advantage of the disaster and victimized an already violated city.

"By and large, the city has been very calm," said police Capt. John Newlin. But reports of "sporadic" looting placed extra pressure on police. District Attorney Arlo Smith said more than 50 people were arrested on felony charges, most on suspicion of looting, burglary and mugging. Prosecutors decided to keep 42 suspects in custody, and the rest were released. "A few individuals want to take advantage of the situation with looting and criminal violence," Smith said. "Those individuals are going to be dealt with tough and firm. We will seek maximum bail and maximum sentences." The suspected looters face prison terms of two to six years if convicted.

Officials said most of the looting was confined to around the Market Street area, where the looters were lured by broken store windows and a nighttime blackout. The crooks were far outnumbered by good Samaritans and people who saw a need and pitched in.

As darkness fell Tuesday over a city without traffic signals and street lights, citizens stood in intersections all over town to direct traffic. "It's the people on the streets, the people with little flashlights; they are the saviors of the city," State Police Lt. Randy Greer said.

"I felt it was my patriotic duty to help out," said Glen Otis, 24, who lives on the streets. As Otis manned his intersection, police drove up, left him some flares and told him to keep up the good work.

Some stores of the Safeway grocery chain

A San Francisco citizen looks up at the twisted remains of some homes and buildings in the Marina District of San Francisco. UPI Photo/Susan Spann

Linda Reed looks over the edge of the collapsed section of the Oakland Bay Bridge hoping for news of her husband, who she thought may have been among the victims trapped when the section of the bridge fell during the earthquake. She did not find her husband among the victims. UPI Photo/J. David Ake

A totally destroyed building and the earthquake buckled street in the Marina District of San Francisco.
UPI Photo/Ron Kuntz

Rescue workers rush to locate and give aid to occupants of automobiles crushed in the collapse of the Cypress section of highway 180 leading to the Oakland Bay Bridge, just following the October 17 earthquake. UPI Photo

A rescue worker and dog search for bodies in the remains of what is left of a three story building in the Marina District of San Francisco following the October 17th earthquake. UPI Photo/Ron Lamkey

President Bush gets a close-up look at the devastation caused by the October 17 earthquake. UPI Photo/L. Mark

A car is crushed under what is left of a home in San Francisco as a result of the October 17th earthquake.
UPI Photo/Rod Lamkey

The remains of automobiles crushed in the collapse of Interstate 880. UPI Photo

John Tranbarger sits on the side of a huge crack in the earth in front of his home in the Santa Cruz mountains. UPI Photo/Dan Groshong

Oakland Athletics baseball player Terry Steinbach comforts his wife just fol-
lowing the earthquake. UPI Photo/Ron Kuntz

Candlestick Park, site of the third game of baseball's World Series, just following the October 17th earth-quake and the cancellation of the baseball game. UPI Photo/Ron Kuntz

This yellow Volkswagen was just one of many automobile casualties on the Cypress section of Highway 180 leading to the Bay Bridge. The deceased occupants of the car are still inside. UPI Photo/Terry Wing

A door mat is about all that is left of value of this home in the Santa Cruz mountains. The center of the earthquake is believed to be near this spot. UPI Photo/J. David Ake

A para-rescue team from Moffett Field, California, lowers a body that was found trapped in a car on the Cypress section of the approach to the Bay Bridge. UPI Photo/Terry Wing.

The Marina District of San Francisco was devastated by the October 17th earthquake. UPI Photo/George Nikiten

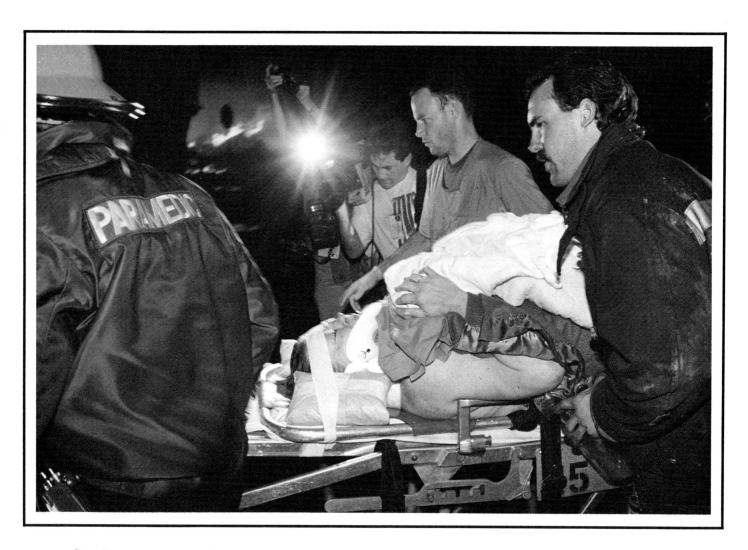

San Francisco paramedics remove a live earthquake victim from one of the damaged buildings near the Marina area. UPI Photo/Susan Spann

This photograph taken just following the earthquake shows people on the Oakland Bay Bridge next to the collapsed section. UPI Photo/Paul Richards

This home, in the Santa Cruz mountains, appears to have been shaken off its foundation and is sliding down the side of the mountain. UPI Photo/J. David Ake

The remains of two automobiles at the collapsed section of the Oakland Bay Bridge. UPI Photo/Dan Groshong

Rescue workers pull damaged autos from a collapsed section of the Oakland Bay Bridge. UPI Photo/ David Ake

Engineers view a small portion of the damaged Cypress section of Interstate 880. UPI Photo/Paul Richards

Rescue workers performing the grim task of removing bodies of people crushed to death when the Cypress section of Interstate 880 collapsed in Oakland. UPI Photo/J. David Ake

Two firefighters survey one of the many earthquake-caused fires on October 17. UPI Photo/Brian Baer

A rescue worker, just following a lengthy effort to revive one of the earthquake victims from the collapse of a section of the Oakland Bay Bridge. UPI Photo/David Ake

Kayakers have a front row seat as work begins on the earthquake-damaged section of the Bay Bridge. UPI Photo/Paul Richards

Baseball legend Joe DiMaggio walks through the Marina District of San Francisco, where he has a home, following the earthquake. UPI Photo/Rod Lamkey

An Oakland Fire Department rescue worker climbs down a hole cut by pneumatic hammers into the top section of the Cypress overpass to get to one of many bodies trapped by the October 17 earthquake. The remains of a trapped motorist are at the center. UPI Photo/Terry Wing

Marina District residents sadly view the fire and destruction of the October 17 earthquake. UPI Photo/ Susan Spann

Rescue workers retrieve a car that "fell" into the collapsed 50-foot section of the Oakland Bay Bridge. UPI Photo/J. David Ake

Military Police guard the Marina District, hard hit by the earthquake. Note the cracks in the building. UPI Photo/Fred Brown

President Bush views the collapsed section of the Oakland Bay Bridge from a government helicopter on October 20. UPI Photo/L. Mark

San Francisco Giant baseball player Brett Butler leads his family off the field at Candle-stick Park just following the earthquake. UPI Photo/Ron Kuntz

Workmen repair earthquake-damage in section 53 of Candlestick Park, site of the World Series on October 17. UPI Photo/Ron Kuntz

What do you put the street sign on when nothing is left standing? Note the auto-mobile crushed under what remains of a building. UPI Photo/George Nikiten

A police officer looks down from a top section of the Cypress section of Interstate 880 at a collapsed section of highway that crushed motorists and automobiles on the highway's bottom section. UPI Photo/Martin Jeong

This photograph shows what hundreds of streets and paved areas now look like in the San Francisco Bay Area following the earthquake of October 17. UPI Photo

With power still out in many downtown San Francisco hotels and office build-ings, Henry Lenz of CBS Radio reads by candlelight about the devastation of the October 17 earthquake. UPI Photo/Paul Richards

A policeman instructing people to clear the area near a marina area fire. UPI Photo/Susan Spann

A National Guardsman walks past what remains of a three story apartment complex in the Marina District. UPI Photo/Rod Lamkey

A building, severely damaged in the Marina District of San Francisco, is supported by lumber to prevent further damage. UPI Photo/Paul Richards

Overhead lines of the municipal trolley bus are cut down on Divisidero Street in the Marina section of San Francisco. Note the remnants of an earthquake-demolished building at the bottom of the picture. UPI Photo/Rod Lamkey

A view of the Oakland Bay Bridge and the San Francisco skyline from Treasure Island, close to the area of the bridge section that collapsed during the October 17 earthquake. UPI Photo/Dan Groshong

Workmen beginning the removal of the collapsed section of the Oakland Bay Bridge. UPI Photo/Paul Richards

Living in a backyard tent because her rented home was destroyed by the October 17th earthquake, Gail Goldenbirdsong and her brother cope with putting their lives back together. UPI Photo/Elizabeth Karnazes

Ford's Department Store is heavily damaged by the October 17th earthquake. UPI Photo/Brian Baer

Loraine Helm and her children, Desirée, Jeff (c) and Marc (r) hold a press conference at Highland Hospital after visiting Buck Helm, her former husband, who was pulled from the earthquake rubble in the collapse of the Cypress section of Interstate 880, caused by the October 17th earthquake. UPI Photo/Martin Jeong

sponding to treatment," said physician Michael Smith, who rode to the hospital with Helm. "He asked for milk," said Smith, smiling.

Helm's car was completely hidden from view until the crack opened, said Oakland Police Capt. Jim Hahn. Oakland Fire Department spokesman Greg Guyan said Helm's cries apparently had not been heard by audio equipment and dogs used to seek survivors because the windows on one side of his compact car were not broken by the crash.

Helm's rescue buoyed the spirits of tired, ragged crews at I-880. As he was lifted from the span and waved his arms, a cheer went up from the workers, who quickly resumed their search with renewed hope.

Oakland, Ca., (UPI),
By Art McGinn, *October 21, 1989*

In what was called a miracle, a survivor was pulled from the rubble of a collapsed freeway Saturday, a little more than three days after the double-decker structure buckled during a devastating earthquake.

"The first thing he said was 'Thank God I'm alive'," said rescue worker Jeff Breckenridge. "Suprisingly, he was moving his arms around. The workers are still up there cheering," he said.

"I raised my hands and screamed and thanked God he was alive," said his ex-wife, Lorene Helm. Mrs. Helm said she heard the news on television at their home in Weaverville, which is located in northern California's remote Trinity County. "Our hopes were getting pretty dim, but we knew, if anyone could make it, it was Buck," said Mrs. Helm, who added that her husband has "a lot of will." While meeting with reporters, Mrs. Helm broke down and left the microphones.

Oakland Mayor Lionel Wilson was on the collapsed structure when workers pulled Helm free. "He waved his arms as he was being brought out," Wilson said. "It was an incredible, wonderful sight to see."

Helm, a ship's clerk, was rushed to Oakland's Highland Hospital and listed in guarded but stable condition. He also had a skull fracture.

Mission San Juan Bautista, Ca., (UPI), By William H. Inman, UPI National Reporter, *October 22, 1989*

Tuesday's killer quake toppled Our Lady of Atonement, sent chandeliers whirling to the ground and opened cracks throughout one of California's most famous missions.

But dizzying experiences are nothing new for Mission San Juan Bautista, bordering the dreaded San Andreas Fault. Alfred Hitchcock filmed "Vertigo" here.

"Hitchcock set up mirrors to make the spiral (belltower) staircase seem to wind on and on," said the Rev. Max Santa Maria, the bespectacled Basque-born rector of the largest of all California's Spanish missions. "Jimmy Stewart had to climb like a madman, even though the real stairs are about 10-feet high," he said. "It was all Hollywood: smoke and mirrors."

In contrast, the 6.9 temblor geologists call the Loma Prieta Earthquake was no special effect. When it struck shortly after 5 p.m. Tuesday, Santa Maria, 50, was almost knocked off his feet in the rectory. Santa Maria dashed to the sanctuary in time to see black dust drop like a storm cloud from the wood-plank ceiling 45 feet up. Iron chandeleirs spun like tops. Saints teetered on their pedestals.

"You felt the hand of God," he said. "It was a spiritual thing."

The hand struck with more force in the 1906 earthquake that devastated San Francisco. Both outer naves, or aisles (the sanctuary includes three) collapsed. They were not rebuilt until the 1970s.

Grizzled and hunched, Servio (Spanish for "Servant") Riviero, 82, who tends the votive candles, felt many of the earlier temblors. He thought Tuesday's was the greatest. "I was sitting down on a stool but it made me stand and take a couple of steps," he said. "I wasn't sure I'd ever sit down again. I thought the walls might tumble again."

But the adobe church proved to be a bastion. It was built well. Rawhide straps fastened rafters for flexibility. Baptistry walls were built 5-feet thick.

The structure was raised by Franciscan friars on the Feast Day of St. John the Baptist on June 24, 1797. The site was considered ideal: 90 miles South of San Francisco, in a valley walled by the Gavilan ("Sparrow Hawk") Range and the Dead Hills, where the soil was deep and the indigenous Indian population friendly. The Indians already worshipped the spirits that shook the earth.

But the location had a big drawback. Cutting through the mission's holiest ground, the unmarked graves of 4,300 Spanish and pioneer settlers, runs an artery of the San Andreas, a fault line dividing North American and Pacific crustal plates, a zone of quakes.

The mission's community of nuns believes it was the presence of Our Lady of Atonement, one of the mission's holiest relics, that protected the church from greater damage. "Our Lady was first seen by a novice," said Sister Carmelita Heredia, 50. "She saw it in a dream. It was 1937." A 4-foot statue was created, based on the vision. The virgin, robed in blue and gold, bears a jeweled crown. She clutches the infant Christ who holds a globe. The nuns took their name from the vision, Sisters of Our Lady of Atonement.

When the quake hit, the virgin fell from her altar in a private sanctuary. Made of plaster, she should have smashed into a thousand pieces. She didn't.

"The infant lost a bit of a foot and the Virgin's (crown) broke," said Sister Heredia. "But God was kind. He showed us his strength and power. He always shows us his mercy."

San Francisco, Ca., (UPI),

By William D. Murray, *October 17, 1989*

Like thousands of other San Franciscans, I sat in Candlestick Park and nervously awaited Game 3 of the 1989 World Series when suddenly the Earth moved. Amazingly, most of the 60,000-plus gathered for the game remained calm and in fact cheered the powerful quake jokingly before realizing that this was no lighthearted matter.

Phones immediately went out and the sky went dark from power outages. Despite harrowing circumstances, no panic swept the stands. Fans stood looking at each other wondering what to do. The gaiety normally associated with a World Series game had turned to fear.

Each aftershock caused concern to grow more and more, and then word began to filter through the crowd on the radios: a section of the Bay Bridge had collapsed. A massive fire was sweeping through the Marina District. The Berkeley Library was on fire. There were deaths.

When Baseball Commissioner Fay Vincent called off the game indefinitely, the order was given to clear the stadium. Thousands of fans streamed out in an orderly fashion, climbing onto MUNI buses, wondering what awaited them in the city. They did not have to wait long.

As the buses approached the city, they were met by streams of workers pouring into neighborhoods. Their faces told a story of worry, anxiety and the awful truth that the unthinkable happened that San Francisco had once again felt the jolt of a mighty earthquake.

As the sun set, the city darkened by the massive power outages took on a ghostly hue.

Only sporadic lights dotted the famed San Francisco skyline, but mostly there was darkness and the amber glow of automobile tail lights.

The eerie wail of sirens pierced the air as emergency crews were pushed to the brink and helicopters landed within blocks of City Hall. What was once only a plan on paper now had turned into an earthquake command center.

With communications slowly returning, the casualty toll would grow and many in the city would go to bed Tuesday night not knowing the fate of their loved ones, who had been stranded elsewhere.

The Davies Symphony Hall oddly glowed like a lit jewel in the middle of the darkness. Inexplicably, its lights were on where there were no other lights for miles.

And the Goodyear blimp hovered above, flashing its advertisements as if nothing had happened.

World Reacts, (UPI),

By Michael Molinski, *October 18, 1989*

The Soviets compared Tuesday's earthquake to last year's temblor in Armenia and offered their help, Pope John Paul II offered his prayers, and the Japanese, many with relatives and business interests in the area, swamped overseas switchboards as the world reacted to earthquake-ravaged California.

"The feelings of the American people at this moment are especially close and understandable for the Soviet people, who have recently experienced the pain of bereavement in Armenia," Soviet Foreign Ministry spokesman Gennady Gerasimov told reporters in Moscow Wednesday.

"To the visitors from California, and in particular from San Francisco, I give the assurance of my prayers for the victims of yesterday's earthquake," the pope said Wednesday in a direct address to some 100 Californians who were among 6,000 pilgrims and tourists attending his weekly general audience at the Vatican. He called the disaster an "immense tragedy" and added, "May almighty God receive the souls of the dead in his peace, and comfort the injured with divine strength."

Offers of condolence and pledges of financial and other assistance flowed in from around the globe.

U.N. Secretary-General Javier Perez de Cuellar sent a message to President Bush expressing his "utmost sadness." "Allow me to extend to you and through you to the bereaved families and to those injured my heartfelt condolences and sympathy," Perez de Cuellar said. "The thoughts of the world are with you and with the people of California at this difficult time."

Prime Minister Rajiv Gandhi of India called President Bush from New Delhi and "conveyed his deepest sympathy at the tragic loss of life in the earthquake," the Press Trust of India reported.

In Paris, French President Francois Mitterrand sent a message to Bush expressing his "sadness and solidarity," and the French Foreign Ministry set up a hot line to help inform French citizens who have relatives in the San Francisco area.

Telegrams of condolence also flowed in from the leaders of several other nations, including Israel, South Korea, Britain, Egypt, and West Germany.

Moscow directed the Soviet ambassador to Washington, Yuri Dubinin, to contact the Bush administration and offer assistance from the Kremlin, Gerasimov said.

Soviet physicians, who were aided by American equipment and staff after the Armenian earthquake, offered whatever assistance they could provide to northern California. The offer came in a telex to the Boston offices of the International Physicians for Prevention of Nuclear War, a Soviet-American organization that

won the 1985 Nobel Peace Prize and that was involved in shipping medical equipment to Armenia. "The natural disaster in the San Francisco Bay area, which led to tragic loss of human lives, is a matter of great concern and compassion among Soviet IPPNW physicians. Please remain assured that if necessary your Soviet colleagues are ready to extend any sort of assistance and cooperation," wrote Mikhail Kuzin, director of the surgical clinic at First Moscow Medical School.

The earthquake was front-page news around the globe.

In Sydney, Australia, the Daily Mirror printed pictures and text about the earthquake across its first five pages. The "Daily Mirror Girl," a bikini-clad beauty which routinely attracts readers to Page 3, was banished to Page 7 for the first time in 30 years.

Expressed in current terms, the losses arising from the 1906 earthquake would be $6.9 billion. Since then, however, insured values have risen substantially and California officials estimate that an earthquake as severe as that in 1906 would cause damage amounting to $31 billion, of which $12 billion would be caused by fire.

Damaging aftershocks possible,
(UPI), By Rob Stein, Science Writer, *October 18, 1989*

The earthquake that rocked northern California was not the fabled "Big One" but uncorked more stress on the infamous San Andreas Fault that will probably trigger aftershocks for some time, experts said. "I'm sure the people who were in this earthquake will say, 'Yes, this was the Big One'," said Russ Needham, a geophysicist at the U.S. Geological Survey's National Earthquake Information Center in Golden, Colo. "But compared to the earthquakes that can occur in this area, like the one in 1906, no this was not the 'Big One'."

Earthquakes are caused by sudden surges from the constantly moving plates beneath the Earth's surface. Tuesday's quake occurred along the San Andreas Fault, which lies between the Pacific Plate and the North American Plate, which are constantly moving in opposite directions. Stress tends to build up between the plates along faults because the plates do not move evenly in all areas. Earthquakes occur when the stress gets so great the plates jerk to relieve the built-up energy, experts said.

"One side slips very suddenly and there is a sudden jerky motion between the ground on one side relative to the other side," said Thomas Jordan, a seismologist at the Massachusetts Institute of Technology in Cambridge, Mass. Although scientists can measure stress along a fault, they have not found good ways to predict when an earthquake will occur because the final trigger for quakes remains a mystery, he said.

The best scientists can do is search for patterns in the earthquake history of an area and try to project the future based on those patterns. But this is very unspecific because there are no good early-warning signs. A quake about the size of Tuesday's had been projected as a strong possibility within 30 years. "It's not like the weather; you can't predict it," said Needham.

The California earthquake occurred Tuesday along a segment of the San Andreas Fault about 10 miles northeast of Santa Cruz, 18 miles south of San Jose and 50 miles southeast of San Francisco. The quake measured 6.9 on the Richter scale, about equal to the temblor that devastated Soviet Armenia in 1988, killing at least 23,000 people. But it was one-tenth the magnitude of the quake that devastated San Francisco in 1906. The 1906 quake also apparently ruptured a much greater length of the fault, Jordan said. "I wouldn't call it the 'Big One' because of that," said Jordan.

Aftershocks of varying frequency and intensity usually follow earthquakes as the geology reacts to the sudden shift from the quake and continues to release stress, experts said. The shocks usually decrease in intensity but can occur for days, weeks or even years following an earthquake. More than 1,400 aftershocks were recorded following Tuesday's initial temblor but most were too small to be felt. The largest aftershock measured 4.7 and was recorded within the first hour after the quake while another aftershock that measured 4.0 was recorded about 10 hours later.

Data from the past 50 years of earthquake history in California suggest there is as much as a 20 percent chance of an aftershock of magnitude 6 or larger (large enough to do further damage) in the first 24 hours after the main shock. The likelihood diminishes thereafter, officials said. "Usually the largest earthquake happens first," said Douglas Wiens of Washington University in St. Louis. "If you had a large earthquake like this, then this is usually the main one. That is not always the case. Occasionally you will have another large earthquake following one like this."

"There will no doubt sometime in the future be an earthquake in that part of (northern) California which rivals the earthquake of 1906," Jordan said. Experts warned that major quakes remain a threat in California even in the aftermath of Tuesday's jolt.

Southern California, which last experienced a major earthquake in 1857, faces an even better chance of the "big one" recurring in the near future, USGS geologist Darrell Herd said in Washington. The Richter scale was not invented then, but it is believed the huge earthquakes of 1857 and 1906 were on the order of magnitude 8. In the meantime, additional earthquakes with magnitudes in the 6-7 range are likely to occur in the San Andreas fault system on an average of once a decade, Herd said.

The same area where Tuesday's earthquake struck produced a magnitude 5.2 earthquake on Aug. 8, as well as a magnitude 5.1 quake in June 1988. Those were the first two significant events along that area of the San Andreas Fault in 70 to 80 years.

Quakes Can Hit Many Areas,
(UPI), By Vincent Del Guidice, *October 17, 1989*

California has a history of deadly earthquakes, but many regions of the United States have suffered equally violent temblors, including Alaska, Massachusetts, and Missouri.

The great San Francisco quake and fire of April 18, 1906, killed more than 700 people, while a quake in Long Beach, Calif., on March 10, 1933, killed 115, and a temblor in San Fernando, Calif., on Feb. 9, 1971, claimed 65 lives, according to the U.S. Geological Survey.

"Many people assume that earthquakes are primarily confined to the West Coast when, in fact, more than 70-million Americans in 44 states are at some risk from earthquakes," the Federal Emergency Management Agency warns.

"Three of the most severe U.S. Earthquakes occurred not on the West Coast, but in the East and Midwest: in Charleston, South Carolina, in 1886; at Cape Anne, Massachusetts, in 1775; and in New Madrid, Missouri, in 1811-1812," the agency said.

The most famous U.S. quake outside of California struck Prince William Sound, Alaska, on Good Friday, March 27, 1964, registering a magnitude of 8.4 on the Richter scale, the second strongest in the world in the 20th century. "The Alaska earthquake triggered extensive landsliding and generated a tsunami," a huge wave, the U.S. Geological Survey said. "It caused an estimated $311 million in damage in Anchorage and south-central Alaska and killed 131 people."

The most violent series of earthquakes to rock the nation, however, struck between 1811 and 1812 along the New Madrid fault in Missouri. There were reports it caused church bells to toll in Washington, D.C. "Three earthquakes hit the New Madrid seismic zone in southeast Missouri and northeast Arkansas December 16, 1811, and January 23 and February 7, 1812, at estimated magnitudes of 8.4 to 8.7," the geological survey said. "Damage and casualties were not great because the area was sparsely populated, but the earthquakes were felt over the entire United States east of the Mississippi River and probably far to the west," the survey said. "The earthquakes caused extensive changes in the surface of the land."

Other major U.S. quakes:

Cape Ann, Massachusetts, Nov. 18, 1755: Centered 200 miles east of Cape Ann, this earthquake of magnitude 6.0 was felt over 400,000 square miles, from Nova Scotia to the Chesapeake Bay and from Lake George, N.Y., east to the Atlantic seaboard. Reported damage: 100 chimneys in Cape Ann and Boston.

Charleston, So. Carolina, Aug. 31, 1886: Sixty people died in an earthquake measuring 6.6 Most buildings in Charleston were destroyed. There was $20 million in damage. The quake was felt from Milwaukee to Havana.

Charleston, Missouri, Oct. 31, 1895: This quake struck with a 6.2 magnitude near the junction of the Ohio and Mississippi rivers, and was felt in 23 states over 1 million-square miles in the strongest quake in the New Madrid seismic region since the quakes of 1811 and 1812.

Mona Passage, Puerto Rico, Oct. 11, 1918: A tsunami spawned by this quake of magnitude 7.5 drowned scores of people. Final death toll placed at 116, with damage estimated at $4 million.

Olympia, Washington, April 13, 1949: Eight people were killed and many were injured in quake of 7.1 magnitude that caused heavy damage in Washington and Oregon and was felt as far as western Montana.

Hebgen Lake, Montana, Aug. 17, 1951: At least 28 people in a resort area were killed in a quake of magnitude 7.3. A landslide blocked Madison River canyon creating a large lake. Summer homes and highways were wiped out. Massive waves pounded shores of Hebgen Lake for 12 hours.

Tallahassee, Fl., (UPI),
By Jeffrey Schweers

Florida, probably the most earthquake-free state in the United States, still felt the effects of the destructive earthquake in the San Francisco area, a state geologist said Wednesday.

The water level of the Florida Aquifer System fluctuated 3 inches, said Ed Lane, a geologist with the Florida Geological Survey of the Department of Natural Resources. A water level recorder in a steel-cased well in the back parking lot of the Survey's office in Tallahassee recorded the sloshing Tuesday night, Lane said. The change was temporary, lasting only a few minutes and having no consequences for residents. "We don't get all quakes, but we do get the larger ones," Lane said.

San Francisco, Ca., (UPI),
October 23, 1989

The city of San Francisco is "alive and well" is the message the Convention and Visitors Bureau hopes to get across with a video presentation being taped over the weekend.

Bureau President John A. Marks had crews on the streets taping segments for what he characterized as a "Charles Kuralt-type" tour to show the world that not all of San Francisco was in ruins.

"Just to remind people that San Francisco is alive and well and open for business," Sharon Rooney of the bureau said.

October is typically one of the busiest months for tourism in San Francisco. But the

Oct. 17 earthquake forced the cancellation of conventions, caused tourists to check out of downtown hotels in droves and may have frightened away thousands of potential visitors.

"But that's to be expected," Bob Begley of the San Francisco Hotel Council said Saturday. "We went through this in the late 1950s (after a good-sized 1957 quake), and business picked up after about a week."

Begley said if the World Series, suspended by the quake, resumes Tuesday as expected, hotel occupancy rates should return to normal, in the 70 to 80 percent range.

While San Francisco hotels are near empty, those in outlying areas, particularly in the north Bay Area, the least affected by quake damage, are full.

"We have been at 100 percent occupancy since about an hour after the quake," said Greg Hardwicke, a manager at the Holiday Inn in San Rafael, about 20 miles north. "It's rather unfortunate but most of our recent check-ins have been people who have lost their homes."

At the Westin St. Francis, an 85-year-old landmark hotel on Union Square, occupancy had dropped to 30 percent. "People were leaving rapidly in great numbers Wednesday," spokeswoman Molly Blaisdell said.

San Francisco's newest hotel, the 1,500-room Marriott Hotel, called "The Jukebox" by locals because of its rounded, mirrored façade, staged its grand opening celebration the day before the quake.

As of the weekend, 600 rooms were occupied. Many of the empty rooms were to have been rented to people attending an Oct. 22 convention by the automaker Nissan. That meeting was scrapped.

"Nissan felt this wouldn't be a good time to introduce their new automobile (the Infiniti line) with a celebration like they'd planned," Rooney said.

Hotels were not the only businesses affected by the exodus of tourists. Taxi drivers, who were in extreme demand the night of the quake as mass transit systems were paralyzed, now find themselves short on fares.

"They all either got on planes and hightailed it out of here or headed for hotels out of town," one dispatcher said.

It will take months to determine just what impact the quake had on the tourism and convention industry. Last year more than 2 million tourists spent 33.3 billion in San Francisco.

The Richter Scale, (UPI),
October 17, 1989

The Richter scale measures the inherent strength of an earthquake at the center of the earthquake. There is, theoretically, no upper or lower limit to the Richter scale.

The highest recorded number was 8.9 from a quake off the coast of Ecuador in 1906 and from a quake off the coast of Japan in 1933.

Every increase of 1 on the Richter scale, for example from magnitude 5.5 to magnitude 6.5, means the ground motion is 10 times greater.

According to the Richter scale, the potential for temblor damage in a populated area is:

Magnitude minus 3: lowest quakes ever recorded.

Magnitude 2: Lowest quake normally felt by humans.

Magnitude 3.5: Quake can cause slight damage.

Magnitude 4: Quake can cause moderate damage.

Magnitude 5: Quake can cause considerable damage.

Magnitude 6: Quake can cause severe damage.

Magnitude 7: A major earthquake, capable of widespead, heavy damage.

Magnitude 8: A "great" earthquake, capable of tremendous damage.

Magnitude 8.9: Highest ever recorded.

Major Earthquakes, (UPI),
October 18, 1989

Three U.S. earthquakes claimed more than 100 lives each:

April 18-19, 1906 San Francisco quake and fire killed 700

March 10, 1933 Long Beach, Calif., quake killed 120 people.

March 27, 1966 Alaska quake killed 114 people.

Other major U.S. quakes:

Nov. 23-24, 1987 Southern California. Temblors measuring 6.2 and 6.6 on the Richter scale shook the Imperial Valley in San Diego County, Calif., injuring at least 94 people in California and Mexico and causing some $4 million damage.

Oct. 1, 1987 Southern California. A quake centered in Montebello, 5.9 on the Richter scale, and a 5.3 aftershock Oct. 4, killed eight people. State officials (on 1-12-88) put damage at $358 million.

July 8, 1986 Southern California. A quake on the Banning fault 12 miles northwest of Palm Springs, 5.9 on the Richter scale, injured 40 people and caused an estimated $5.75 million damage.

April 24, 1984 Northern California. A quake 12 miles southeast of San Jose, measuring 6.2 on the Richter scale, injured 25 people. The quake was said to be the strongest on Calaveras fault since 1911 and only the fourth in the San Francisco Bay area to register over 6.0 since the 1906 San Francisco quake.

Oct. 28, 1983 Northwest. A quake called the strongest to hit the contiguous 48 states since 1959, measuring 6.9 on the Richter scale, hit eight northwestern states and Canada, killing two children with falling debris in Challis, Idaho.

May 2, 1983 Central California. A quake at Coalinga near Fresno, measuring 6.5 on the Richter scale, injured 47 people and caused an estimated $31 million damage, leveling the town's eight-block business section.

Jan. 24-27, 1980 Northern California. Nine separate quakes along the Greenville fault 35 miles southeast of San Francisco, registering up to 5.6 on the Richter scale, shook buildings 150 miles away. No fatalities were reported.

Aug. 6, 1979 Northern California. A quake centered at Hollister, 100 miles south of San Francisco on the Calaveras fault, measuring 5.9 on the Richter scale, was called the strongest earthquake in the region in at least 50 years. No major injuries or damage were reported.

Feb. 9, 1971 Southern California. A quake in the Los Angeles area, measuring 6.5 on the Richter scale, killed 64 people, 43 of them at a VA hospital. Hundreds were injured and damage was estimated at more than $1 billion. Officials counted nearly 1,000 buildings with major damage and 139 unsafe for occupancy.

March 27, 1964 Southern Alaska. A quake centered 105 miles east of Anchorage, measuring 8.4 on the Richter scale, killed 114 people. Damage was estimated at $750 million. The most powerful quake recorded in North America, it created a 12-foot wave at Crescent City, Calif., that killed 12 people.

Aug. 17-20, 1959 Montana. A quake at West Yellowstone, Montana, killed 28 people and injured about 60, mainly vacationers, measuring 7.3 on the Richter scale.

July 21-22, 1952 Southern California. Two quakes in two days killed 14 people. One quake centered at Tehachapi south of Bakersfield, measuring 7.8 on the Richter scale, killed 12 people and destroyed or damaged 150 homes July 21. Two more people died in a quake at Bakersfield July 22.

Worst Earthquakes, (UPI),
October 17, 1989

A list of the 10 worst earthquakes in history by loss of life:

1.	January	24, 1556	Shensi, China	830,000
2.	October	11, 1737	Calcutta, India	300,000
3.	May	20, 526	Antioch, Syria	250,000
4.	July	28, 1976	Tangshan, China	242,000
5.	May	22, 1927	Nan-shan, China	200,000
6.	September	1, 1923	Tokyo, Japan	140,000
	(including quake and subsequent fire and tidal wave)			
7.	December	30, 1730	Hokkaido, Japan	137,000
8.	December	16, 1920	Kansu, China	100,000
9.	September	27, 1290	Chihli, China	100,000
10.	March	1201	Aegean Sea	100,000

San Francisco, Ca., (UPI),
By Peter Rapalus, *October 20, 1989*

At least two aspects of living in earthquake country make the sudden shifting of the Earth's plates possibly more terrifying than any other natural disaster. One is their unpredictability. There is no way to determine when a quake will hit, making preparedness sometimes luck more than anything else. Wary residents can strengthen their house foundation, pack away supplies and drinking water and learn CPR.

But no amount of preventive action could have helped the motorists who were crushed by the collapse of the upper deck of a stretch of Interstate 880 in Oakland from the Loma Prieta earthquake.

Earthquakes are also highly erratic. Most times they are light and do no damage. Then there was the devastation caused Tuesday.

A 6.9 magnitude earthquake had never struck the Marina District of San Francisco since part of the bay was reclaimed and houses were built there. So its residents had no test of their sandy soil and vulnerable water table. The ground composition of the Marina District played a major role in the amount of destruction Loma Prieta caused in the posh neighborhood.

When the quake struck at 5:04 p.m. Tuesday, the water table rose into the sandy ground, causing it to rise, fall, shift, and sway more violently than in other areas of San Francisco. The area's dominant style of buildings, most dating back to the 1930s, also contributed to its massive damage.

"We know where the most damage came: the three- to four-story building built over garages," said Frank Moss, a city engineer. "The garages aren't built well enough to support a whole building."

"One of the worst problems there is (that) most of the buildings have a 'soft' story," said Ron Gallagher, a structural engineer who advises local governments on post-quake inspection guidelines. By "soft story," he meant weak first floors, usually garages, on apartment buildings. When converting stately houses to multi-unit rental buildings, he said, "They put the apartment units above the ground floor and the heavy walls were taken out and replaced by garage doors. When the ground shakes, you don't have very much strength at floor level," Gallagher said. In contrast to the apartment buildings that slid into the streets, many single-family homes in the area, also built over garages, survived relatively intact, because they stopped at one above-garage level.

He said there are two primary types of quake damage caused to buildings: from shaking and from its effects on the soil. Soil damage is usually responsible for the most dramatic destruction and carnage.

Almost as elusive as earthquake prediction is sure-fire earthquake protection, although advances made in recent decades appear to have been right on target. Virtually all of San Francisco's skyscrapers sustained very minor or no damage. The high-rises are built on huge roller and spring super-systems that allow them to roll with the punch rather than buckle and break. "We've learned a lot from previous earthquakes and we'll learn a lot from this one," Moss said.

The learning process began as soon as the earth stopped shaking from the initial quake (aftershocks have been numerous). The U.S. Geological Survey, which experienced a seven-hour power outage and minor damages at its offices in Menlo Park, sent teams out along known faults to search for surface faulting and other scientific clues.

The agency had sobering news for quake-shocked people who think they have gotten past the fabled "Big One." "The rupture of this 30-mile-long segment of the San Andreas fault has not reduced the assessment that there is a 50 percent chance for one or more magnitude-7 earthquakes in the San Francisco Bay Area in the next 30 years," the USGS reported. On the bright side, the USGS said, the chances of a repeat of the magnitude-8.3 quake that leveled San Francisco in 1906 was "less than 10 percent." Which means it could happen in 10 years, in a century or in a millenium. Or today.